GATEWAY TO

GERMAN DICTION

Teacher's Supplementary Materials

John Glenn Paton

Das deutsche Alphabet
[das dɔøtʃə alfabeːt]

das A	[aː]		N	[ɛn]
das B	[beː]		O	[oː]
C	[tseː]		P	[peː]
D	[deː]		Q	[kuː]
E	[eː]		R	[ɛr]
F	[ɛf]		S	[ɛs]
G	[geː]		T	[teː]
H	[haː]		U	[uː]
I	[iː]		V	[faʊ]
J	[jɔt]		W	[veː]
K	[kaː]		X	[ɪks]
L	[ɛl]		Y	[ʏpsilɔn]
M	[ɛm]		Z	[tsɛt]

das ß, scharfes S
[ɛstsɛt, ʃarfəs ɛs]

der Umlaut
[ʊmlaʊt]

B-flat Major	*B-Dur*	[beːduːr]
B-flat Minor	*B-Moll*	[beːmɔl]
B Major	*H-Dur*	[haːduːr]
B Minor Mass	*H-Moll-Messe*	[haːmɔl mɛsə]

German Diction Resources

In addition to books listed in the bibliography, page 124, *Gateway to German Diction*, the following resources are recommended for your library.

A fine general dictionary, using IPA for both German and (British) English:
THE OXFORD-DUDEN GERMAN DICTIONARY, revised. Oxford: Clarendon Press, 1997.

For translations of song texts (no IPA):
THE RING OF WORDS, An Anthology of Song Texts, by Philip L. Miller. New York: W. W. Norton, 1973. Highly recommended, drawn from the poets' original versions. Includes other languages.

GERMAN LIEDER, by Philip L. Miller. New York: Continuum, 1990. Drawn from *The Ring of Words*, with addition of other poems.

LIEDER LINE BY LINE, and Word by Word, revised edition, by Lois Phillips. Oxford: Clarendon Press, 1996. Both idiomatic and word-by-word translations.

WORD BY WORD TRANSLATIONS OF SONGS AND ARIAS, Part I, German & French, by Berton Coffin and others. German translations by Werner Singer. New York: Scarecrow Press, 1966. The only book listed here that includes German operatic arias.

PENGUIN BOOK OF LIEDER, by Siegbert S. Prawer. Middlesex: Penguin, 1964.

THE FISCHER-DIESKAU BOOK OF LIEDER, selected and introduced by Dietrich Fischer-Dieskau, translations by Bird and Stokes. New York: Limelight Editions, 1984. Large collection, more than 750 song texts.

SCHUBERT: THE COMPLETE SONG TEXTS, translated by Richard Wigmore. New York: G. Schirmer, 1988.

THE SINGER'S SCHUMANN, edited, with introductions and translations, by Thilo Reinhard. New York: Pelion Press, 1989. Excellent material on 92 selected songs by Schumann.

Some recommended books about song interpretation and the history of lieder are:
THE NINETEENTH-CENTURY GERMAN LIED, by Lorraine Gorrell. Portland: Amadeus Press, 1993. Acknowledges Fanny Mendelssohn Hensel and other women composers.

POETRY INTO SONG, Performance and Analysis of Lieder, by Deborah Stein and Robert Spillman. New York: Oxford University Press, 1996.

THE GERMAN LIED AND ITS POETRY, by Elaine Brody and Robert A. Fowkes. New York University Press, 1971.

Consistency and Contrast Exercises

Speak the German words in each exercise out loud. First, speak the words in vertical columns with a consistent pronunciation of the focus vowels. Then speak the words in horizontal rows with clear contrasts between the focus vowels.

(In general, only one meaning is given for words with multiple meanings.
Operatic roles are identified only with "role.")

Exercise 1:

[iː]	[ɪ]	[eː]	[ɛ]
bieten [biːtən] (to offer)	bitten [bɪtən] (to ask)	beten [beːtən] (to pray)	das Bett [bɛt] (bed)
das Lied [liːt] (song)	litt [lɪt] (suffered)	der Athlet [atleːt] (athlete)	die Ländler [lɛntlər] (country waltz)
der Trieb [triːp] (compulsive desire)	Tristan [trɪstan] (role)	treten [treːtən] (to step)	die Treppe [trɛpə] (staircase)
wir [viːr] (we)	wirr [vɪr] (confused)	wer [veːr] (who)	der Wärter [vɛrtər] (watchman)

Exercise 2:

[eː]	[ɛː]	[ɛ]	[ɑː]
das Meer [meːr] (ocean)	Mär [mɛːr] (fable)	merkt [mɛrkt] (takes notice)	mahnt [mɑːnt] (warns)
die Feder [feːdər] (feather)	die Väter [fɛːtər] (ancestors)	der Vetter [fɛtər] (cousin)	der Vater [fɑːtər] (father)
die Seele [zeːlə] (soul)	die Säle [zɛːlə] (concert halls)	selten [zɛltən] (seldom)	der Saal [zɑːl] (concert hall)
wen [veːn] (whom)	wähnt [vɛːnt] (imagines)	wenn [vɛn] (if)	der Wahn [vɑːn] (illusion)

Exercise 3:

[uː]	[ʊ]	[oː]	[ɔ]
der Mut [muːt] (courage)	die Mutter [mʊttəɾ] (mother)	die Mode [moːdə] (fashion)	das Moll [mɔl] (minor key)
die Kuh [kuː] (cow)	die Kunst [kʊnst] (art)	kost [koːst] (caresses)	die Kost [kɔst] (food)
sucht [zuːxt] (seeks)	die Sucht [zʊxt] (craving)	das Solo [zoːlo] (solo)	Isolde [izɔldə] (role)
Schubert [ʃuːbəɾt] (composer)	der Schluss [ʃlʊs] (end)	der Schoß [ʃoːs] (lap, womb)	schoss [ʃɔs] (shot, past tense)

Exercise 4:

[oː]	[ɔ]	[ɑː]	[a]
tot [toːt] (dead)	toll [tɔl] (insane)	tat [tɑːt] (did)	die Taste [tastə] (piano key)
dem Sohne [zoːnə] (to the son)	die Sonne [zɔnnə] (sun)	die Sahne [zɑːnə] (cream)	besann [bəzan] (thought it over)
holen [hoːlən] (to fetch)	hocken [hɔkən] (to crouch)	Hagen [hɑːgən] (role)	hacken [hakən] (to hoe)
Wotan [voːtan] (role)	Wozzeck [vɔttsɛk] (role)	waren [vɑːɾən] (were)	warten [vaɾtən] (to wait)

Exercise 5:

[iː]	[yː]	[uː]
die Biene [biːnə] (bee)	die Bühne [byːnə] (stage)	die Buhle [buːlə] (mistress)
vier [fiːɾ] (four)	für [fyːɾ] (for)	fuhr [fuːɾ] (led)
fliegen [fliːgən] (to fly)	der Flügel [flyːgəl] (grand piano)	der Flug [fluːk] (flight)
trieft [triːft] (trickles)	trüb [tryːp] (gloomy)	der Trug [truːk] (deception)

Exercise 6:

[ɪ]	[ʏ]	[ʊ]
binden [bɪndən] (to tie)	die Bünde [bʏndə] (alliances)	der Bund [bʊnt] (alliance)
das Kissen [kɪsən] (cushion)	küssen [kʏsən] (to kiss)	der Kuss [kʊs] (kiss)
Liszt [lɪst] (composer)	die Lüste [lʏstə] (pleasures)	die Lust [lʊst] (pleasure, joy)
Richard [rɪçart] (name)	der Rücken [rʏkən] (back)	der Rucksack [rʊkzak] (backpack)

Exercise 7:

[eː]	[øː]	[oː]
flehte [fleːtə] (pleaded)	die Flöte [fløːte] (flute)	der Floh [floː] (flea)
die Kehle [keːlə] (throat)	der König [køːnɪç] (king)	die Kohle [koːlə] (coal)
heben [heːbən] (to lift)	hören [høːɾən] (to hear)	oben [oːbən] (up above)
das Thema [teːma] (theme)	die Töne [tøːnə] (tones)	der Ton [toːn] (tone)

Exercise 8:

[ɛ]	[œ]	[ɔ]	[a]
äffen [ɛfən] (to ape)	öffnen [œfnən] (to open)	offen [ɔfən] (open)	die Affen [afən] (apes)
die Mächte [mɛçtə] (powers)	möchte [mœçtə] (would like)	mochte [mɔxtɛ] (did like)	die Macht [macht] (power)
stecken [ʃtɛkən] (put)	die Stöcke [ʃtœkə] (batons)	der Stock [ʃtɔk] (baton)	stark [ʃtark] (strong)
westlich [vɛstlɪç] (western)	östlich [œstlɪç] (eastern)	der Osten [ɔstən] (east)	der Ast [ast] (branch)

Exercise 9:

[yː]	[ʏ]	[øː]	[œ]
üben [ˈyːbən] (practise)	üppig [ˈʏpɪç] (voluptuous)	öd [øːt] (barren)	öffentlich [ˈœffəntlɪç] (public)
lügen [ˈlyːgən] (to lie)	die Lücke [ˈlʏkə] (gap)	lösen [ˈløːzən] (to solve)	löschen [ˈlœʃən] (to extinguish)
die Tür [tyːr] (door)	die Türme [ˈtʏrmə] (towers)	die Törin [ˈtøːrɪn] (foolish woman)	der Töpfer [ˈtœpfər] (potter)
kühn [kyːn] (bold)	die Künste [ˈkʏnstə] (arts)	die Königin [ˈkøːnɪgɪn] (queen)	köstlich [ˈkœstlɪç] (delightful)

Exercise 10:

[iː]	[ae]	[ɑo]	[ɔø]
schien [ʃiːn] (seemed)	der Schein [ʃaen] (light)	schauen [ˈʃɑoən] (to look)	scheu [ʃɔø] (shy)
ihnen [ˈiːnən] (to them)	einen [ˈaenən] (to unite)	außen [ˈɑosən] (outside)	äußerst [ˈɔøsərst] (extreme)
trieben [ˈtriːbən] (propelled)	treiben [ˈtraebən] (to propell)	die Traube [ˈtrɑobə] (grape)	treu [trɔø] (faithful)
hieß [hiːs] (was named)	heiß [haes] (hot)	das Haus [hɑos] (house)	Tannhäuser [ˈtanhɔøzər] (role)

Exercise 11:

[ʃ]	[ç]	[x]	[k]
der Tisch [tɪʃ] (table)	dich [dɪç] (to you)	das Fach [fax] (vocal category)	der Tag [tɑːk] (day)
der Mensch [mɛnʃ] (human being)	der Mönch [mœnç] (monk)	sacht [zaxt] (quietly)	sagt [zɑːkt] (says)
die Nische [ˈniːʃə] (niche)	nicht [nɪçt] (not)	die Nacht [naxt] (night)	nackt [nakt] (naked)
der Busch [bʊʃ] (bush)	die Bäche [ˈbɛçə] (brooks)	der Bach [bax] (brook, composer)	der Bock [bɔk] (billy-goat)

Name _____

Opera Game

These are the names of German operas and some of their characters, written in IPA.
Can you guess (or do you know?) how to spell and pronounce these names?

1. [di ʔɛntfyːruŋ ɑos dem zeraʲel]_____

2. [konstantsə] _____

3. [diː tsɑobərfløːtə] _____

4. [di køːnɪgɪn der naxt] _____

5. [der fraeʃʏts] _____

6. [di maestərzɪŋər fon nʏrnbɛrk] _____

7. [valtər fon ʃtɔltsɪŋ]_____

8. [der rɪŋ dɛs niːbəluŋən] _____

9. [di gœtərdɛmməruŋ] _____

10. [di fleːdərmɑos] _____

11. [der rozənkavaliːr] _____

12. [di fɛltmarʃalɪn,prɪntsɛsɪn fon vɛrdənbɛrk] _____

13. [di frao oːnə ʃatən] _____

14. [di lʊstɪgə vɪtvə]_____

ANSWERS: 1. *Die Entführung aus dem Serail* (*Abduction from the Seraglio* by Mozart). 2. Konstanze (soprano in no. 1). 3. *Die Zauberflöte* (*The Magic Flute* by Mozart). 4. Die Königin der Nacht (soprano in no. 3). 5. *Der Freischütz* (*The Freeshooter* by Weber). 6. *Die Meistersinger von Nürnberg* (*The Master Singers of Nuremberg* by Wagner). 7. Walther von Stolzing (tenor in no. 9). 8. *Der Ring des Nibelungen* (*The Ring of the Nibelung* by Wagner). 9. *Die Götterdämmerung* (*The Twilight of the Gods* by Wagner). 10. *Die Fledermaus* (*The Bat* by Johann Strauss, Jr.). 11. *Der Rosenkavalier* (*The Rose Cavalier* by Richard Strauss). 12. die Feldmarschallin, Prinzessin von Werdenberg (soprano, known as "the Marschallin," in no. 11). 13. *Die Frau ohne Schatten* (*The Woman without a Shadow* by R. Strauss). 14. *Die lustige Witwe* (*The Merry Widow* by Lehar).

Name _____

READING GUIDE to Chapter 1: Phonetic Concepts

As you read *Gateway to German Diction* you will find the answers to the following questions.

Diction Related Concepts

When we make our sung texts clear, we have good (1) _____. When we speak or sing only the best, most correct sounds, we have good (2) _____. When we speak or sing efficiently and with little tension, we have good (3) _____. Our aim is to achieve good (4) _____.

The science of speech sounds is (5) _____, and the scholars who study it are (6) _____. Speech sounds that help to determine the meaning of what we say are called (7) _____. Whether a particular sound determines meaning in a particular language is demonstrated by means of (8) _____. Sounds that are produced in physically different ways but are accepted by the listener as being equivalent to each other are called (9) _____.

Orthography Related Concepts

The writing and spelling of a language constitute its (10) _____. Words that are identical in meaning are (11) _____. Words that look identical are (12) _____. Words that sound identical are (13) _____.

If two letters are used to spell one sound, they are called a (14) _____. A letter written twice is doubled, but a consonant articulated twice is (15) _____.

Syllable Related Concepts

The strongest syllable of a word is said by phoneticians to be (16) _____, rather than "accented." The standard IPA method of indicating a strong syllable is to add the sign (17) [___] before the syllable. *Gateway to German Diction* uses a different method, underlining the vowel of the stressed syllable. Within a syllable or word, a vowel or consonant can be in any of three locations: (18) _____. A consonant that occurs between two vowels is said to be (19) _____.

Vowel Related Concepts

Vowel phonemes use the vocal tract (the voice-producing instrument from the vocal cords upwards) as a

(20) _____. Vowels are formed with a free flow of the

(21) _____. In order to describe a vowel in comparison to other vowels, we must

know (22) _____ (how many?) pieces of information.

"Bright vowels" are formed primarily by action of the (23) _____. "Dark vowels" are

formed primarily (at least in singing) by action of the (24) _____. Vowels for which both

(23) and (24) are active are called (25) _____. They are shown in German orthography

by a diacritic called an (26) _____, but that sign is not used in IPA transcriptions.

Some vowels are perceived as lying between bright and dark, but are not mixed; they are described as

(27) _____.

Instead of "close, mid, open" *Gateway to German Diction* recognizes "levels" or degrees of openness

for various vowels. German requires us to recognize (28) _____ (how many?) levels. German also

requires us to recognize vowel lengths: long and short.

Diphthong Related Concepts

A diphthong contains two vowels, but the listener perceives and accepts them as (29) _____.

An English diphthong may be shown by a single letter like "I"; a German diphthong is always shown by

(30) _____ (how many?) letters. In contrast to a diphthong, a single vowel sound may be called a

(31) _____.

In all German diphthongs, the main vowel always comes (32) _____. The weaker vowel

always comes (33) _____ and is called a(n) (34) _____.

How many semi-vowels does German have? (35) _____! When foreign words with semi-vowels

are used in German, the semi-vowels become (36) _____.

Consonant Related Concepts

Consonant phonemes all involve some degree of obstructing, stopping or diverting the

(37) _____. In order to describe a consonant in comparison to other consonants,

we must know (38) _____ (how many?) pieces of information.

Consonants formed while the vocal folds are vibrating are said to be (39) _____. Such consonants are part of our singing because they have (40) _____. Consonants that do not use vocal fold vibration are said to be (41) _____.

Consonants are articulated in various ways; those that block the air only for a brief instant are called (42) _____. A consonant that is released with an audible burst of air is said to be (43) _____. If a stop consonant and a sibilant are articulated at the same time, the result is called an (44) _____.

Consonants are articulated in various places in the mouth. Three areas of the tongue, named from front to back, are (45) _____. The ridge behind the upper teeth is called the (46) _____ ridge. The roof of the mouth has two areas, the (47) _____ and (48) _____. Behind the palate hangs the (49) _____.

Diction Related Concepts
ANSWERS: (1) diction. (2) pronunciation. (3) articulation. (4) communication.
(5) phonetics. (6) phoneticians. (7) phonemes. (8) minimal pairs. (9) allophones.

Orthography Related Concepts
ANSWERS: (10) orthography. (11) synonyms. (12) homonyms.
(13) homophones. (14) digraph. (15) geminated.

Syllable Related Concepts
ANSWERS: (16) stressed. (17) [']. (18) initial, medial or final. (19) intervocalic.

Vowel Related Concepts
ANSWERS: (20) resonator. (21) breath, air. (22) three. (23) tongue.
(24) lips. (25) mixed. (26) umlaut. (27) central. (28) five.

Diphthong Related Concepts
ANSWERS: (29) one. (30) two. (31) monophthong. (32) first. (33) second.
(34) offglide, vanish vowel. (35) none. (36) non-syllabic vowels.

Consonant Related Concepts
ANSWERS: (37) breath. (38) three. (39) voiced. (40) pitch. (41) voiceless. (42) stops.
(43) aspirated. (44) affricate. (45) tip, blade and body *or* apex, lamina and dorsum. (46) alveolar.
(47) hard palate. (48) soft palate. (49) uvula.

Name _____

READING GUIDE to Chapter 2: The German Language

Germanic Languages and German Dialects

German and English both belong to the large (1) _____ family of languages.

Germany, Austria and Switzerland all use an official language that, in English, is called

(2) _____. People who inhabit one limited area may speak an

alternative form of a language known as a (3) _____.

    The particular form of German that is used in theaters and opera houses is based on the pronouncing

dictionary named after Dr. Theodor (4) _____. Another important authority for

pronunciation is the dictionary known as (5) _____.

    German poetry uses many words that originated in other languages; they are called

(6) _____.

ANSWERS: (1) Germanic. (2) high German. (3) dialect. (4) Siebs. (5) Duden. (6) loan words.

Name _____

READING GUIDE to Chapter 3: Characteristic Patterns and Sounds in German

What Makes German Sound German?

Compared to English, the energy level of spoken German is (1) _____. Just as in English,

most syllables end with consonants and are said to be (2) _____. Romance

languages prefer smooth connections between syllables and words, but German prefers

(3) _____ even more than English does. German has strong

(4) _____, while French has practically none at all. Compared to Romance languages,

German consonants are more numerous and are used more for (5) _____.

Just as in English, German P, T and K sounds are (6) _____.

How German Words are Formed— Grammatical Endings

The basic, underlying meaning of a German word is contained in the (7) _____. A longer

German word usually consists of various parts called (8) _____. German uses many

grammatical endings, which indicate the word's (9) _____ in the sentence. These

typically contain the weak vowel called a (10) _____. Participles all begin with the

prefix (11) _____.

Syllabication of Simple Words

In a simple word a medial consonant joins to the (12) _____ _____. If a long

vowel precedes a medial H, it is usually (13) _____.

When there are two or more consonants between syllables, the syllables are divided before

(14) _____. Instead of the spelling KK, German uses (15) _____. In older

texts the correct syllabication of the word *dicker* would be (16) _____.

(Notice: According to an international agreement, after 1999 the correct syllabication is *di-cker*.)

Syllable Separation Before Vowels

Most German words begin (and end) with a (17) _____. When a word of any

importance begins with a vowel the IPA may show a separation with the symbol:

(18) [___]. This may also happen within a word if the syllable after a prefix begins with a

(19) _____.

Do You Have to Make a Glottal Stop?

The space between the two vocal folds is the (20) _____. That space is (21)

_____ for breathing, but it closes to prepare for (22) _____.

In a so-called "glottal stop" the vocal folds are (23) _____ until air pressure blows them apart.

What Makes German Sound German?
    ANSWERS: (1) higher. (2) closed. (3) separation.
    (4) stresses. (5) expression. (6) aspirated.

How German words are formed— Grammatical endings
    ANSWERS: (7) root. (8) elements.
    (9) function. (10) schwa. (11) ge-.

Syllabication of Simple Words
    ANSWERS: (12) following syllable. (13) silent.
    (14) last consonant. (15) CK. (16) dik-ker.

Syllabic Separation Before Vowels
    ANSWERS: (17) consonant. (18) [?]. (19) vowel.

Do You Have to Make a Glottal Stop?
    ANSWERS: (20) glottis. (21) open. (22) singing. (23) closed.

Name _____

READING GUIDE to Chapter 4: Short and Long Vowels

What is Vowel Length?

We are used to thinking that short and long English vowels have different qualities, but they may also take a

different amount of (1) _____. In English, vowel duration alone never determines

meaning, that is, it is not (2) _____. Some short English vowels are always followed by

(3) _____. Misuse of vowel duration by a foreigner contributes to the impression

that the person has an (4) _____.

How Vowel Length Works in German

A German child learns vowel length while learning to talk and later learns the rules of

(5) _____. We reverse the process. In the IPA a long vowel is shown by adding

(6) [_____] after the vowel symbol. (Short vowels have no special marking.)

Why Must Singers Understand Vowel Length?

In German there are pairs of words (minimal pairs) that have different meanings and are distinguished from

each other only by vowel length. This proves that length is (7) _____.

Imagine two notes of equal length; if the vowel fills up almost the entire length of the note, we will

understand that it is (8) _____. If a consonant fills up the latter part of the note, we will

understand that the vowel is (9) _____. Vowels that are different in length may

also be different in (10) _____. In considering how length and quality affect

understandability, the more important factor is (11) _____.

Vowel Quality, Vowel Length and Syllabic Stress

In stressed syllables, any vowel letter can stand for either a short or a long vowel. If the short and long pro-

nunciations have different qualities, then the short pronunciation is more (12) _____ than the

long one. A long vowel is usually more (13) _____ than the short one.

Up to 60% of unstressed syllables contain the weak vowel, (14) [___], which is called by the name

(15) _____. Of the remaining unstressed syllables, most are spoken with vowels that

are both (16) _____ and (17) _____.

How Spelling Indicates Vowel Length

Pick a word from the following list and write it next to the appropriate rule: *das Meer* (ocean), *offen* (open), *leben* (to live), *hinter* (behind), *viel* (much), *der Stroh* (straw), *in* (in), *das Rad* (plural: *die Räder*, wheel)

L (a) A doubled vowel letter is pronounced LONG.   18. _____

L (b) A vowel at the end of a stressed syllable is LONG.   19. _____

L (c) IE is pronounced LONG.   20. _____

L (d) A vowel followed by H in the same syllable is LONG.   21. _____

L (e) In a one-syllable word before a single consonant if longer forms

      of the word exist, the vowel is LONG.   22. _____

S (a) Before a double consonant, a vowel is SHORT.   23. _____

S (b) Before two consonants in the same root, a vowel is SHORT.   24. _____

S (c) Before a final consonant in a short word of only one form,

      a vowel is SHORT.   25. _____

Problem Areas Related to Vowel Length

If a stressed vowel precedes certain letters, we have to use a dictionary to check length. These letters

include (26) _____, _____, and _____.   Also if a word ends with two or more consonants, they may be the

grammatical ending of a (27) _____.

What is Vowel Length?
ANSWERS: (1) time. (2) phonemic. (3) consonants. (4) accent.

How Vowel Length Works in German
ANSWERS: (5) spelling. (6) [ː].

Why Must Singers Understand German Vowel Length?
ANSWERS: (7) phonemic. (8) long. (9) short. (10) quality. (11) length.

Vowel Quality, Vowel Length and Syllable Stress
ANSWERS: (12) open.   (13) higher/ more closed. (14) [ə]. (15) schwa.
(16) short. (17) open.

How Spelling Indicates Vowel Length
ANSWERS: (18) Meer. (19) leben or Räder. (20) viel. (21) Stroh. (22) Rad. (23) offen. (24) hinter. (25) in.

Problem Areas Related to Vowel Length
ANSWERS: (26) CH, SS and ß. (27.) verb.

Name _____

READING GUIDE to Chapter 5: Individual Vowel Sounds

Individual Vowel Sounds

The German language uses (1) _____ (how many?) vowel sounds. In the chart on page 35 the vowels

shown near the bottom of the box are more (2) _____ than vowels near the top. Vowels are

classified by (3) ____(how many?) degrees of openness. Vowels at the left of the chart have sound

qualities that we describe as (4) _____, and they are formed primarily by lifting the

(5) _____ toward the front of the mouth. The vowels on the right, which we describe as

(6) _____, are formed primarily by rounding the lips. Both actions are performed

simultaneously for a group of vowels that we do not have in English, called (7) _____.

In IPA we write the symbol [ː] after a vowel to show that it is (8) _____.

Of all the vowels used in German, (9) _____ are usually long, two vary in length, and (10) _____

are always short.

The vowels in English "man, sung, worth" are (11) _____ used in German.

Bright Vowels

Acoustically, the bright vowels all have strong high (12) _____. Physically, they are all

produced by lifting the (13) _____ to some degree. If desired, the tip of the tongue may always

be kept behind (14) _____.

[iː] and [ɪ]

The English vowel called "long E," as in "green," is shown in IPA by the symbol (15) [___]. The English

vowel called "short I," as in "grin," is shown in IPA by (16) [___]. In German both vowels are spelled

with the letter (17) ____.

English speakers often make the mistake of changing [iː] to a diphthong before the letters (18) _____

or _____.

Three spellings that are nearly always pronounced [iː] are (19) _____, _____, and _____.

The definite article, "the," has various forms in German, which vary according to the number and gen-

der of the noun and its function in the sentence. By far the most common word spelled with IE is the article

die, which uses the vowel (20) [___]. It is used before feminine nouns when they are subjects or direct

objects and before all plural nouns.

[eː], [ɛ] and [ɛː]

The English diphthong called "AY," as in "say," does not exist in German; the closest corresponding

German sound is the long vowel (21) [___].   The English vowel called "short E," as in "set," is shown in

IPA by (22) [___]. In German both of these vowels are normally spelled with the letter (23) _____.

The sound of [ɛ] can be spelled with a different letter and an umlaut, this way: (24) _____. The same

letter is also used when [ɛ] is a long vowel, transcribed: (25) [___]. The letter Ä can always be substituted

with the spelling (26) _____. The spelling ÄH can be substituted with the spelling (27) _____.

The definite article, "the," before a masculine singular noun may have four different forms. It is

worthwhile to memorize them because they occur so often in German texts of all kinds. (They also have

other functions; for instance, *der* is also used for all genders in the plural possessive.) Using IPA, indicate

the vowel quality of each one:

("the," subject)	*der*	(28) [___]	
("the," possessive)	*des*	(29) [___]	
("the," indirect object)	*dem*	(30) [___]	
("the," direct object)	*den*	(31) [___]	

Because they are unstressed, the vowels in all articles, regardless of their quality, are (32) _____.

[ɑː] and [a]

These vowels are distinguished much more by length than by color. They are spelled with the letter (33) _____.

The longer vowel can also be spelled with the letters (34) _____.

[ə]

Final E in English often shows that the preceding vowel is long (examples, "robe, rode, rogue"), and it is

usually silent. Final E in German indicates nothing about the preceding vowel, and it is always pronounced

(35) [___]. This vowel is also used in other weak syllables, for example, the prefixes GE- and BE-, and

also (36) _____ and _____ .

This symbol has a name derived from Hebrew: (37) _____. We sing this vowel a great

deal because the occurrence of schwas is equal to nearly (38) _____ of all German vowels.

Dark Vowels

Acoustically, the dark vowels all lack strong high (39) _____. Physically, they are all

produced by the (40) _____ to some degree. If desired, the tip of the tongue

may always be kept behind (41) _____.

[uː] and [ʊ]

As in the case of [ɑː] and [a], these two vowels are distinguished more by length than by color. They are

both spelled with the letter (42) _____. The longer vowel can be spelled with the letters (43) _____.

Notice that in the loan word *Musik*, the first syllable has the sound of "moo" and not of "mew."

[oː] and [ɔ]

The English diphthong called "long O," as in "Oh!," does not exist in German; the closest corresponding

German sound is the long vowel (44) [___], but it is much (45) _____ in color. The English

vowel called "short O," as in "pot," does not exist in German at all.

What Germans call *offenes O* (open O) is similar to British AW. The symbol for it is (46) [___], and it

is always short. Many North Americans never use this vowel at all, and those who use it seldom darken it

as much as Germans do. The correct way to darken vowels is to (47) _____.

These vowels are very different from each other both in length and color. Both are spelled with the let-

ter (48) _____. The longer vowel may also be spelled with the letters (49) _____.

Mixed Vowels

The four German mixed vowels have (50) _____ action of the lips and tongue. If an

Umlaut is not available, Ü can be replaced with the letters (51) _____ and Ö can be replaced with the

letters (52) _____.

[yː] and [ʏ]

The sound of [yː] uses the same tongue position as (53) [_____]. Its symbol, called

(54) _____, has a straight diagonal line and extends below the line of writing.

The sound of [ʏ] uses the same tongue position as (55) [_____]. Its symbol, called

(56) _____, has a vertical line for the bottom half and may also have a horizontal

stroke (called a serif) at the bottom.

These vowels are distinguished more by length than by color. They are both spelled with the letter
(57) _____ or, if an umlaut is not available, the letters (58) _____. The longer vowel may also be spelled
with the letters (59) _____ or, if an umlaut is not available, (60) _____.

[øː] and [œ]

The sound of [ʏː] uses the same tongue position as (61) [_____]. Its symbol is called

(62) _____.

　　The sound of [û] uses the same tongue position as (63) [_____]. Its symbol is called

(64) _____.

　　These vowels are very different from each other both in length and color. Both are spelled with the
letter (65) _____ or, if an umlaut is not available, the letters (66) _____. The longer vowel may also be
spelled with the letters (67) _____ or, if an umlaut is not available, (68) _____.

French Nasalized Vowels in German

Nasal resonance is created by lowering the (69) _____. In German and English no
vowels are nasal, all vowels are (70) _____, with only a little added nasal resonance. Not all
Germans know how to produce French nasalized vowels, but educated speakers are expected to do so when
appropriate. Orthographically, all French nasals are spelled with a vowel letter followed by either of two
consonant letters (71) _____ or _____.

Non-syllabic Vowels

In words of Germanic origin most syllables contain one vowel (monophthong), although two letters may be
used in the spelling. If a syllable contains two vowel sounds, they form a (72) _____,
and the stronger of the two will always be the (73) _____. In other cases of two consecutive vowel
letters, they probably stand for vowels that are in two different (74) _____.

　　In loan words, on the other hand, there may also be cases in which the first of two consecutive vowel
letters stands for a vowel that is not sustained. It is formed momentarily before the articulators move on to
form the second vowel. Such a vowel is said to be (75) _____. In IPA it is shown
by an added marking, a diacritic, in this case a (76) _____. Such vowels are
pronounced as in the language of origin.

Individual Vowel Sounds
ANSWERS: (1) fourteen. (2) open. (3) five. (4) bright. (5) tongue.
(6) dark. (7) mixed. (8) long. (9) six. (10) six. (11) never.

Bright Vowels
ANSWERS: (12) overtones. (13) tongue. (14) the lower teeth.

[iː] and [ɪ]
ANSWERS: (15) [i:]. (16) [ɪ]. (17) I. (18) R, L. (19) IE, IH, IEH. (20) [i:].

[eː], [ɛ] and [ɛː]
ANSWERS: (21) [e:]. (22) [ɛ]. (23) E. (24) Ä. (25) [ɛ:].
(26) AE. (27) AEH. (28) [e]. (29) [ɛ]. (30) [e]. (31) [e]. (32) short.

[ɑː] and [a]
ANSWERS: (33) A. (34) AH.

[ə]
ANSWERS: (35) [ə]. (36) suffixes and grammatical endings. (37) schwa. (38) 1/3.

Dark Vowels
ANSWERS: (39) overtones. (40) rounding the lips. (41) the lower teeth.

[uː] and [ʊ]
ANSWERS: (42) U. (43) UH.

[oː] and [ɔ]
ANSWERS: (44) [o:]. (45) darker. (46) [ɔ]. (47) round the lips. (48) O. (49) OH.

Mixed Vowels
ANSWERS: (50) simultaneous. (51) UE. (52) OE.

[yː] and [ʏ]
ANSWERS: (53) [i:]. (54) Lower-case Y. (55) [ɪ]. (56) Small Capital Y.
(57) Ü. (58) UE. (59) ÜH. (60) UEH.

[øː] and [œ]
ANSWERS: (61) [e:]. (62) slashed O. (63) [ɛ].
(64) O-E ligature. (65) Ö. (66) OE. (67) ÖH. (68) OEH.

French Nasalized Vowels in German
ANSWERS: (69) soft palate. (70) oral. (71) M or N.

Non-sylabic Vowels
ANSWERS: (72) diphthong. (73) first. (74) syllables. (75) non-syllabic. (76) small curved line.

Name _____

READING GUIDE to Chapter 6: Diphthongs

The number of diphthongs in *Hochdeutsch* is only (1) _____, and there are no triphthongs. English has many more diphthongs, so we have to consciously avoid certain diphthongs that we are accustomed to. For instance, where German requires [eː] we may accidentally say the English diphthong (2) [____]. Where German requires [oː] we may say the English diphthong (3) [____]. And Hochdeutsch never uses a schwa [ə] in place of R as formal English does in words like: "are, bear, pier, more, pure, fire, sour."

In the IPA, a diphthong is shown with two separate vowel symbols that do not touch each other. If two letter forms are written together as one, they stand for a different sound. For instance, [ae] is a diphthong but [œ] is the symbol for the vowel in the word "hat."

[ae]

When this diphthong is sung, the vowel that is prolonged is (4) [____], even though the spelling may not include the letter A. The vanish vowel is (5) [____], which is more (6) _____ than the vanish vowels of the similar diphthongs in Italian and English. Diphthong 1 has four possible spellings:

(7) _____.

[ɑo]

When this diphthong is sung, the vowel that is prolonged is (8) [____], and the spelling includes the letter A. The vanish vowel is (9) [____], which is more (10) _____ than the vanish vowels of the similar diphthongs in Italian and English. Diphthong 2 has only one possible spelling: (11) _____.

[ɔø]

When this diphthong is sung, the vowel that is prolonged is (12) [____], but the spellings do not include the letter O. The vanish vowel is (13) [____], which is more (14) _____ than the vanish vowels of the similar diphthongs in Italian and English. Diphthong 3 has two normal spellings: (15) _____ and _____. If an umlaut is not available, the diphthong might be spelled (16) _____.

About German Dictionaries

Be prepared for the likelihood that your personal German dictionary uses IPA symbols for diphthongs that are different from those learned here. Singers should use the diphthong transcriptions that are used in the dictionary known by the name of the original author, (17) _____, because in those transcriptions the vanish vowels are the most (18) _____.

ANSWERS: (1) three. (2) [ɛɪ]. (3) [oʊ]. (4) [a]. (5) [e]. (6) open. (7) EI, AI, EY, AY.
(8) [ɑ]. (9) [o]. (10) open. (11) AU
(12) [ɔ]. (13) [ø]. (14) open. (15) EU and ÄU. (16) AEU. (17) Siebs. (18) open.

Name _____

READING GUIDE to Chapter 7: Consonants

First, here are a few terms regarding the ways in which consonants occur. If a consonant is at the beginning of a syllable, it is (1) _____. If it occurs between two syllables, it is (2) _____. If it occurs at the end of a syllable, it is (3) _____. If two or more consonants are consecutive in the same syllable, they form a (4) _____.

Nasal Consonants

When we articulate nasal consonants, how much of the breath is diverted through the nose? (5) _____%.

Single and double consonants are pronounced alike in speaking, but in singing, a doubled nasal consonant is prolonged after a vowel that is (6) _____.

The closure that produces [m] is formed physically by (7) _____. In addition to the nose, resonance is felt inside the whole (8) _____.

The closure of [n] is formed by the front edge of the tongue against the (9) _____ and the sides of the tongue against the (10) _____. In addition to the nose, there is a resonating space in the back of the mouth, over the tongue.

The closure of [ŋ] is formed by the back of the tongue against the (11) _____. In addition to the nose, resonance occurs behind the mouth, in the (12) _____. When a German word has NK in a single element, as in *sank*, the N is pronounced (13) [____].

Lateral and Trill Consonants

[l] is called "lateral" because breath passes around the (14) _____ of the tongue.

In speaking a word like "bottle," the second syllable may have only the consonant [l] and no vowel at all. In singing, we have to supply the vowel (15) [___].

Lower-case R [r] symbolizes what kind of R? (16) _____.

Fishhook R [ɾ] symbolizes what kind of R? (17) _____.

Stop Consonants

German has three voiceless stop consonants: (18) [___, ___, ___]. Just as in English, they are pronounced with an audible burst of air, that is, they are (19) _____.

German has three voiced stop consonants: (20) [___, ___, ___]. In initial and medial positions they are also pronounced just as in English, but in final position they are changed into consonants that are (21) _____.

The closure for [p] or for [b] is made between (22) _____. The closure for [t] or for [d] is made between the tongue and (23) _____. The closure for [k] or for [g] is made between the back of the tongue and (24) _____.

If a voiced stop letter is in final position or is combined with other consonants in a final cluster, it is pronounced as if it were voiceless. Therefore, final B is pronounced (25) [____], final D is pronounced (26) [____], and final G is pronounced (27) [____]. This also applies if a voiced stop is combined with other consonants in a final cluster. For instance, final BT is pronounced (28) [____], final GD is pronounced (29) [____].

Fricative Consonants

[f] is the sound of air passing between the lower (30) _____ and the upper (31) _____. In German words [f] is spelled not only with F but also with the letter (32) _____. In loan words from Greek [f] may be spelled (33) _____.

[v] is the same as [f] except that it is (34) _____. In German words [v] is usually spelled with the letter (35) _____. It is also part of the cluster [kv], spelled (36) _____. In loan words [v] is sometimes spelled (37) _____.

Fricative (and Sibilant) Consonants

[s] is the sound of air passing between the front surface of the (38) _____ and the (39) _____. German voiceless [s] never occurs in (40) _____ position. If you see the German letter ß, the consonant is always (41) _____. If you don't have the letter ß available, you can substitute the spelling (42) _____.

Under new spelling rules effective in 1999, an *Eszet*, ß, is used only after long vowels and diphthongs, regardless of the position in the word. It is no longer used in final position after a short vowel, for example, *ich muß* (I must) is now spelled: *ich muss*.

[z] is the same as [s] except that it is (43) _____. [z] is the normal pronunciation of

the letter S in (44) _____ position.

[ʃ] resembles [s] except that the channel through which the breath passes is (45) _____, and

the lips may be rounded. The normal spelling of [ʃ] is (46) _____, except in a case where the letters CH

belong to the suffix (47) _____. In loan words from French, [ʃ] is spelled with (48) _____.

If you see the spelling SH, you know that the word is a (49) _____.

The cluster SP in initial position is pronounced (50) [_____] instead of [sp]. The cluster ST in initial

position is pronounced (51) [_____] instead of [st]. But SP and ST do not have these pronunciations if

they are in (52) _____ position, or if they occur as part of a (53) _____

ending, or if they occur in different parts of a (54) _____ word.

[ʒ] is the same as [ʃ] except that it is (55) _____. [ʒ] occurs in loan words from

French, spelled with the letter (56) _____.

More Fricative Consonants

CH has two possible pronunciations in words of German origin. One pronunciation is heard when the

tongue is lifted in the front of the mouth, as it is for the vowel (57) [____]. The sound of forward CH is

called the *Ich-Laut*, and its IPA symbol is (58) [____]. *Ich-Laut* will be heard whenever CH follows a

vowel other than (59) _____, or when CH follows a diphthong other than (60) _____, or when

CH follows any (61) _____. *Ich-Laut* is also heard when a word ends with the

spelling (62) —_____. If such a word is changed by the addition of an ending that starts with a vowel, the

[ç] changes to (63) [____].

When [C] is voiced, the sound is "curly-tail J," shown by the symbol (64) [____]. (Be sure to make a

loop at the bottom!]

Other than the *Ich-Laut*, the other pronunciation of CH is heard when the tongue is lifted in the back.

This is called the *Ach-Laut*, shown by the symbol (65) [____]. *Ach-Laut* is heard when CH follows

(66) ____, ____ or ____, and only then.

H in initial position is pronounced (67) [___]. If H is used in final position, it is indicating a long

vowel and it is (68) _____. If H appears in medial position, one must decide whether it is

silent, following a long vowel, or pronounced to begin the next syllable. Music publishers always place a

hyphen before a medial H, as in *Ru-he*. It appears that the second syllable begins with H, but the root

syllable is *Ruh-* and the H is silent.

An Affricate, [ts]

When we hear a stop and a fricative pronounced so close together that we hear them as a single sound, that

sound is an (69) _____. Most German sounds of this kind are written with two

alphabet letters, but the single letter Z stands for (70) [____]. At the end of a German word this affricate

can also be spelled (71) _____ or _____. After a stressed short vowel this affricate can be spelled

(72) _____ or _____. In loan words it may be spelled (73) _____ or _____.

ANSWERS: (1) initial. (2) medial. (3) final. (4) cluster.

Nasal Consonants
ANSWERS: (5) 100. (6) short. (7) both lips. (8) mouth.
(9) alveolar ridge or upper teeth. (10) upper teeth. (11) soft palate. (12) oral pharynx. (13) [ŋ].

Lateral and Trill Consonants
ANSWERS: (14) sides. (15) [ə]. (16.) rolled. (17) flipped.

Stop Consonants
ANSWERS: (18) [p t k]. (19) aspirated. (20) both lips. (21) alveolar ridge, teeth.
(22) soft palate. (23) [p] (24) [t]. (25) [k]. (26) [p]. (27) [t]. (28) [k]. (29) [kt].

Fricative Consonants
ANSWERS: (30) lip. (31) teeth. (32) V. (33) PH.
(34) voiced. (35) W. (36) QU. (37) V.

Fricative (and Sibilant) Consonants
ANSWERS: (38) tongue. (39) alveolar ridge. (40) initial. (41) voiceless.
(42) SS. (43) voiced. (44) beginning. (45) wider. (46) SCH. (47) -chen.
(48) CH. (49) compound. (50) [ʃp]. (51) [ʃt]. (52) final. (53) superlative. (54) compound. (55) voiced. (56) G.

More Fricative Consonants
ANSWERS: (57) [i]. (58) [ç]. (59) A, O, U.
(60) AU. (61) consonant. (62) -IG. (63) [g].
(64) [j]. (65) [x].
(66) A, O or U. (67) [h]. (68) silent.

An Affricate
ANSWERS: (69) affricate. (70) [ts]. (71) DS or TS. (72) TZ or ZZ. (73) C or T.

Name _____

WORKSHEET NO. 1: Chapter 4

The following is a list of terms used by musicians and singers.
In each word does the underlined vowel letter stand for a Long or a Short vowel?
Enter "L" or "S" accordingly, along with the letter of one of the rules found on pp. 32–33.

Examples: der Atem (breath)   <u>Lc</u>

bedeckt (covered)   <u>Sa</u>

1. die Fassung (version)   _____

2. die Betonung (accentuation)   _____

3. der Akt (act of a play or opera)   _____

4. der Chor, des Chores (chorus, chorus's)   _____

5. von (of)   _____

6. die Bühne (stage)   _____

7. der Dirigent (conductor)   _____

8. der Sänger (singer)   _____

9. froh (happy)   _____

10. lieblich (sweet)   _____

11. die Oper (opera)   _____

12. Kopfton (head tone)   _____

13. die Seele (soundpost of a violin)   _____

14. der Triller (trill)   _____

15. tief (low)   _____

16. hohe (high)   _____

ANSWERS: 1. Sa. 2. Lc. 3. Sb. 4. Le. 5. Sc. 6. Ld. 7. Sb. 8. Sb.
9. Ld. 10. Lb. 11. Lc. 12. Sb. 13. La. 14. Sa. 15. Lb. 16. Ld.

Name _____

WORKSHEET NO. 2: Chapter 5

Long and Short Vowels, Bright and Central

Notice that throughout these exercises an answer in brackets is an IPA symbol.
Use a German dictionary as needed.

[iː] or [ɪ]?

The symbol [iː] must have a dot over the "i" and the semi-colon lengthener.
The [ɪ] must have its crosspieces (serifs) at top and bottom.

1. [___] nicken (nod)

2. [___] nieder (down)

3. [___] irren (stray)

4. [___] die Miene (facial expression)

5. [___] mitten (in middle)

6. [___] die Mine (land-mine)

7. [___] die Melodie (melody)

8. [___] die Minne (romantic love)

9. [___] das Fieber (fever)

10. [___] ihrer (of her)

11. [___] nichts (nothing)

12. [___] das Gebiet (area)

13. [___] die Stimme (voice)

14. [___] vernichten (annihilate)

[eː] or [ɛ]?

15. [___] nennen (name)

16. [___] leben (to live)

17. [___] setze (set)

18. [___] gelebt (lived)

19. [___] der See (lake)

20. [___] das Bett (bed)

21. [___] die Erde (earth)

22. [___] beten (to pray)

23. [___] weg (away)

24. [___] das Gebet (prayer)

25. [___] das Be (flat sign)

26. [___] sehnen (to long for)

27. [___] der Ersatz (substitute)

28. [___] der Berg (mountain)

29. [___] beste (best)

30. [___] eben (even)

31. [___] der Weg (noun: way)

32. [___] Beethoven

[ɛː] or [ɛ]?

33. [___] gesättigt (satiated)

34. [___] gänzlich (entirely)

35. [___] der Käse (cheese)

36. [___] gefällt (pleases)

37. [___] die Tränen (tears)

38. [___] die Mächte (powers)

39. [___] rückwärts (backwards)

40. [___] der Jäger (hunter)

41. [___] krähen (to crow)

42. [___] die Krähe (crow)

43. [___] wählen (choose)

44. [___] das Mädchen (girl)

[ɑː] or [a]?

45. [___] der Bach (brook)

46. [___] zusammen (together)

47. [___] der Saal (large room)

48. [___] habe (I-have)

49. [___] der Wagner (carriage builder)

50. [___] arm (poor)

[ə]

Draw a circle around each E that stands for a schwa [ə]. There may be more than one in a word.

51. g e g a n g e n (gone).

52. die S o n n e (sun).

53. o f f e n e (open).

54. b e d e c k t (covered).

55. der L e s e n d e (person reading).

56. ü b e r r o n n e n (overflowing).

ANSWERS: (Bright Vowels) 1. [ɪ]. 2. [iː]. 3. [ɪ]. 4. [iː]. 5. [ɪ]. 6. [iː]. 7. [iː]. 8. [ɪ]. 9. [iː]. 10. [iː]. 11. [ɪ]. 12. [iː]. 13. [ɪ]. 14. [ɪ]. 15. [ɛ]. 16. [eː]. 17. [ɛ]. 18. [eː]. 19. [eː]. 20. [ɛ]. 21. [eː]. 22. [eː]. 23. [ɛ]. 24. [eː]. 25. [eː]. 26. [eː]. 27. [ɛ]. 28. [ɛ]. 29. [ɛ]. 30. [eː]. 31. [eː]. 32. [eː]. 33. [ɛ]. 34. [ɛ]. 35. [ɛː]. 36. [ɛ]. 37. [ɛː]. 38. [ɛ]. 39. [ɛ]. 40. [ɛː]. 41. [ɛː]. 42. [ɛː]. 43. [ɛː]. 44. [ɛː] (an exception).

(Central Vowels) 45. [a]. 46. [a]. 47. [ɑː]. 48. [ɑː]. 49. [ɑː]. 50. [a].

These syllables contain [ə]: 51. ge-, -en. 52. -ne. 53. -fe-, -ne. 54. be-. 55. -sen-, -de. 56. -ber-, -nen.

Name _____

WORKSHEET NO. 3: Chapter 5

Long and Short Vowels, Dark and Mixed

Throughout these exercises an answer in brackets is an IPA symbol.
Use a German dictionary as needed.

[uː] or [ʊ]?

The symbol [u] must have the finishing stroke on the right side;
the [U] must be round on the bottom and may have horizontal strokes (serifs) at the top.

1. [___] die Kummer (care)   2. [___] der Zug (train, draft)

3. [___] jubelnd (rejoicing)   4. [___] jung (young)

5. [___] durch (through)   6. [___] die Uhr (hour)

7. [___] der Durst (thirst)   8. [___] die Tugend (virtue)

[oː] or [ɔ]?

9. [___] der Morgen (tomorrow)   10. [___] der Gott (god)

11. [___] doch (indeed)   12. [___] die Rose (rose)

13. [___] sonst (otherwise)   14. [___] wohl (indeed)

15. [___] das Boot (the boat)   16. [___] die Oper (opera)

[yː] or [ʏ]?

The symbol [y:] has a straight diagonal line and extends below the line of writing. [Y] sits on the line and may have a horizontal stroke at the bottom.

17. [___] fühlen (to feel)   18. [___] füllen (to fill)

19. [___] die Lüfte (breezes)   20. [___] der Rhythmus (rhythm)

21. [___] schützen (to protect)   22. [___] blühen (to bloom)

23. [___] das Gemüt (disposition)   24. [___] die Wünsche (wishes)

25. [___] wüsste (would know)   26. [___] die Mühe (trouble)

[øː] or [œ]?

27. [___] zöge (would move)

28. [___] das Köpfchen (dear head)

29. [___] die Höhe (height)

30. [___] schön (beautiful)

31. [___] die Königin (queen)

32. [___] der Schöpfer (creator)

33. [___] der Löffel (spoon)

34. [___] das Röslein (little rose)

35. [___] trösten (to comfort, derived from *Trost*, which has a long vowel)

36. [___] köstlich (precious)

ANSWERS: (Dark Vowels) 1. [ʊ]. 2. [uː]. 3. [uː]. 4. [ʊ] 5. [ʊ]. 6. [uː]. 7. [ʊ]. 8. [uː]. 9. [ɔ]. 10. [ɔ]. 11. [ɔ]. 12. [oː]. 13. [ɔ]. 14. [oː]. 15. [oː]. 16. [oː].

(Mixed Vowels) 17. [yː]. 18. [ʏ]. 19. [ʏ]. 20. [ʏ]. 21. [ʏ]. 22. [yː]. 23. [yː]. 24. [ʏ]. 25. [ʏ]. 26. [yː]. 27. [øː]. 28. [œ]. 29. [øː]. 30. [øː]. 31. [øː]. 32. [œ]. 33. [œ]. 34. [øː]. 35. [øː]. 36. [œ].

Name _____

WORKSHEET NO. 4: Chapter 5

Review of All Monophthong Vowels

1. [___] will (will)

2. [___] öfter (now and then)

3. [___] musste (had to)

4. [___] ihnen (to them)

5. [___] loben (to praise)

6. [___] die Väter (fathers)

7. [___] lebst (livest)

8. [___] die Töchter (daughters)

9. [___] schleppen (to drag)

10. [___] die Hymne (hymn)

11. [___] werden (to become)

12. [___] über (over)

13. [___] voll (full)

14. [___] das Gerät (machine)

15. [___] strahlen (to radiate)

16. [___] hören (to hear)

17. [___] wieder (again)

18. [___] der Band (volume, book)

19. [___] der Duft (fragrance)

20. [___] die Terz (interval of a third)

21. [___] der Schuh (shoe)

22. [___] hinweg (away)

23. [___] vermuten (to suspect)

24. [___] das Ohr (ear)

25. [___] horchen (to listen)

26. [___] die Sünde (sin)

27. [___] die Dämmerung (twilight)

28. [___] die Lyrik (lyric poetry)

29. [___] gewöhnen (to accustom)

30. [___] die Männer (men)

31. [___] bist (thou art)

32. [___] der Teer (tar)

ANSWERS: 1. [ɪ]. 2. [œ]. 3. [ʊ]. 4. [iː]. 5. [oː]. 6. [ɛː]. 7. [e]. 8. [œ]. 9. [ɛ]. 10. [ʏ]. 11. [eː]. 12. [yː]. 13. [ɔ]. 14. [ɛː]. 15. [ɑː]. 16. [øː]. 17. [iː]. 18. [a]. 19. [ʊ]. 20. [ɛ]. 21. [uː]. 22. [ɛ]. 23. [uː]. 24. [oː]. 25. [ɔ]. 26. [ʏ]. 27. [ɛ]. 28. [yː]. 29. [øː]. 30. [ɛ]. 31. [ɪ]. 32. [eː].

Name _____

WORKSHEET NO. 5: Chapter 6. Diphthongs

Transcribe the diphthong. Is it [ae] or [ɑo] or [ɔø]?
(One word contains no diphthong; transcribe the vowel instead.)

1. der Laib (the loaf)   [____]

2. der Leib (the body)   [____]

3. die Beleuchtung (lighting)   [____]

4. schlau (clever)   [____]

5. ziemlich (rather)   [____]

6. versäumen (to lose)   [____]
    (might also be spelled versaeumen)

7. keusch (chaste)   [____]

8. vereint (united)   [____]

9. braun (brown)   [____]

10. scheint (seems)   [____]

11. heulen (to howl)   [____]

12. der Traum (dream)   [____]

13. Bayern (Bavaria)   [____]

14. die Träume (dreams)   [____]
    (might also be spelled Traeume)

15. eins (one)   [____]

16. die Hauptprobe (dress rehearsal)   [____]

Practice with Diphthongs

Transcribe the following words into IPA. All of the vowels were discussed in Chapter 5
and all of the consonants in these words keep their normal alphabet letters in IPA.

17. das Bein (leg)   [_____]   18. meinen (to think) [_____]

19. der Maikäfer   [_____]   20. der Kreis   [_____]
    (May beetle)   (circle)

21. das Haus   [_____]   22. die Laune   [_____]
    (house)   (mood)

23. die Mauer   [_____]   24. gebaut   [_____]
    (wall)   (built)

25. die Freude (joy) [_____]   26. die Eule (owl)   [_____]

27. die Träume   [_____]   28. Bäume (trees)   [_____]
    (dreams)

These are German words that contain diphthongs. How might they be spelled?

29. [aes] (ice cream) _____   30. [bərɔøen] _____
                                                  (to regret)

31. [baom] (tree)   _____   32. [trɔx]   _____
                                                  (faithful)

Here are pairs of similar words; what vowel or diphthong is in the first syllable of each?

33. der Haufen (heap) [____]   34. hoffen (to hope)   [____]

35. das Leid   [____]   36. das Lied (song)   [____]
    (sorrow)

37. Lotte   [____]   38. die Leute (people) [____]
    (girl's name)

39. Lieder (songs)   [____]   40. leider   [____]
                                                  (unfortunately)

ANSWERS: 1. [ae]. 2. [ae]. 3. [ɔø]. 4. [ɑo]. 5. [iː]. 6. [ɔø]. 7. [ɔø]. 8. [ae].
9. [ɑo]. 10. [ae] 11. [ɔø]. 12. [ɑo]. 13. [ae]. 14. [ɔø]. 15. [ae]. 16. [ɑo].
17. [baen]. 18. [maenən]. 19. [maekɛːfər]. 20. [kraes]. 21. [haos]. 22. [lɑonə]. 23. [mɑoər]. 24. [gəbɑot].
25. [frɔødə]. 26. [ɔølə]. 27. [trɔømə]. 28. [bɔømə]. 29. Eis. 30. bereuen. 31. Baum. 32. treu.
33. [ɑo]. 34. [ɔ]. 35. [ae]. 36. [iː]. 37. [ɔ]. 38. [ɔø]. 39. [iː]. 40. [ae].

WORKSHEET NO. 6: Chapter 7, Consonants

Name _____

N and NG

The following words include either [n] or [ŋ]. Indicate which one in the brackets.
(The tail of the symbol [ŋ] should extend below the line.)

1. der Rang (upper balcony)   [____]

2. bedenkt! (consider!)   [____]

3. geschwind (fast)   [____]

4. gesangvoll (melodious)   [____]

5. die Angabe (boasting)   [____]

6. die Gesänge (songs)   [____]

7. sank (sank)   [____]

8. hinkriegt (fixes, sets right)   [____]

Voiceless and Voiced Stops

Give the IPA symbol for the underlined consonant.

9. die Ausgabe (edition)   [____]

10. die Quarte (interval of a fourth) [____]

11. der Bund (guitar fret)   [____]

12. das Xylophon (xylophone)   [____]

13. dämpfen (to mute)   [____]

14. der Fuchs (fox)   [____]

15. das Blatt (page)   [____]

16. decken (to cover)   [____]

17. absolut (absolute)   [____]

18. der Eingang (entrance)   [____]

19. finster (dark)   [____]

20. der Schlag (stroke)   [____]

21. das Doppelbe (double flat sign) [____]

22. schlagen (to strike)   [____]

23. das Glück (happiness)   [____]

24. der Eingang (entrance)   [____]

25. übst (you practice)   [____]

26. gab (gave)   [____]

[f] and [v]

Which IPA transcription is correct, A or B?

27. die Phrase (phrase)   A. [fhrɑːsə]   B. [frɑzə]   _____

28. die Vollendung (completion)   A. [vɔlʔɛnduːŋ]   B. [fɔlʔɛndʊŋ]   _____

29. wieviel? (how much?)   A. [viːfiːl]   B. [fiːʔfiːl]   _____

30. verwechseln (to exchange)   A. [fɛrvɛksəln]   B. [vɛrvɛksɛln]   _____

31. die Quinte (interval of a fifth)   A. [kwɪntə]   B. [kvɪntə]   _____

32. die Volksweise (folktune)   A. [fɔlksvaezə]   B. [fɔlksfaesə]   _____

ANSWERS: (Nasal consonants) 1. [ŋ]. 2. [ŋ]. 3. [n]. 4. [ŋ].
5. [n] (*an-* is a prefix). 6. [ŋ]. 7. [ŋ]. 8. [n] (*hin-* is a prefix).
(Stop consonants) 9. [b]. 10. [k]. 11. [t]. 12. [k]. 13. [p]. 14. [k]. 15. [t]. 16. [k].
17. [p]. 18. [g]. 19. [t]. 20. [k]. 21. [b]. 22. [g]. 23. [k]. 24. [g]. 25. [p]. 26. [p].
([f] and [v]) 27. B. 28. B. 29. A. 30. A. 31. B. 32. A.

Name _____

WORKSHEET NO. 7: Chapter 7, Consonants (continued)

Sibilant Fricatives

The following words include either [s], [z] or [ʃ]. Indicate which one in the brackets. (The symbol [ʃ] must extend below the line.)

1. singen (to sing)   [____]

2. des Betrugs (deceit's)   [____]

3. der Hals (neck)   [____]

4. dem Halse (to the neck)   [____]

5. lösen (to loosen)   [____]

6. nass (damp)   [____]

7. die Nässe (dampness)   [____]

8. die Nase (nose)   [____]

9. Hänsel (operatic role)   [____]

10. der Auszug (moving out)   [____]

11–12. sass (sat)   [____], [____]

13. stellen (to put)   [____]

14. die Gestalt (appearance)   [____]

15.   die Schule (school)   [_____]

16.   der Todestag (day of death)   [_____]

17.   beste (best)   [_____]

18.   erste (first)   [_____]

19–20. erstens (at first)   [_____], [_____]

21.   leichteste (lightest)   [_____]

22.   austeilen (pass out, distribute)   [_____]

23.   Lieschen (dear Lisa)   [_____]

24–25. die Glasscherbe (sliver of glass) [_____], [_____]

26–27. die Tagessuppe (soup of the day) [_____], [_____]

28–29. dasselbe (the same)   [_____], [_____]

Here is a German tongue-twister:

Ein Student mit Stulpenstiefeln stand auf
einem spitzen Stein, staunte still und stöhnte,
stolperte und starb.
(A student with high top boots stood on a
pointed stone, marveled quietly and groaned,
stumbled and died.)

ANSWERS: 1. [z]. 2. [s]. 3. [s]. 4. [z]. 5. [z]. 6. [s]. 7. [s]. 8. [z].
9. [z]. 10. [s]. 11. [z]. 12. [s]. 13. [ʃ]. 14. [ʃ]. 15. [ʃ]. 16. [s].
17. [s]. 18. [s]. 19. [s]. 20. [s]. 21. [s]. 22. [s]. 23. [s]. 24. [s].
25. [ʃ]. 26. [s]. 27. [s]. 28. [s]. 29. [z].

Name _____

WORKSHEET NO. 8 : Chapter 7, Consonants (concluded)

Fricatives, Concluded, and an Affricate [ts]

Which IPA transcription is correct, A or B?

1. das Echo (echo)   A. [ɛkhɔ]   B. [ɛço]   _____

2. flüchten (to flee)   A. [flʏçtən]   B. [flʏxtɛn]   _____

3. jodelt (yodels)   A. [joːdəlt]   B. [joːdlət]   _____

4. lachen (to laugh)   A. [laçən]   B. [laxən]   _____

5. hoch (high)   A. [hoːx]   B. [hɔç]   _____

6. Ochs (ox)   A. [ɔks]   B. [ɔkʃ]   _____

7. das C (letter c, key of C)   A. [tseː]   B. [sɛ]   _____

8. die Sitzprobe (seated rehearsal) A. [sɪttsproːbə]   B. [zɪtsproːbə]   _____

9. das Orchester (orchestra)   A. [ɔrxɛʃtər]   B. [ɔrkɛstər]   _____

10. das Cis (c-sharp)   A. [tsɪs]   B. [siːs]   _____

11. die Eiche (oak)   A. [aeʃɛ]   B. [aeçə]   _____

12. feucht (damp)   A. [fɔøçt]   B. [fɔɪxt]   _____

13. des Rauchs (smoke's)   A. [rauʃ]   B. [raoxs]   _____

14. suchen (to seek)   A. [suːçən]   B. [zuːxən]   _____

15. Liebchen (darling)   A. [liːpçən]   B. [liːbxən]   _____

16. mancher (some)   A. [maːnxər]   B. [mançər]   _____

17. prachtvoll (glorious)   A. [praxtfɔl]   B. [praxtvɔl]   _____

Transcribe (Use a dictionary if necessary):

18. fluchen (to curse)   [_____]

19. sechs (six)   [_____]

20. Schütz (composer's name)   [_____]

21. das Wachs (wax)   [_____]

22. des Lichts (light's)   [_____]

23. rächen (to avenge)   [_____]

24. der Charakter (role)   [_____]

25. melancholisch (melancholy) [_____]

26. Cäcilie (name)   [_____]

ANSWERS: 1. B. 2. A. 3. A. 4. B. 5. A. 6. A. 7. A. 8. B. 9. B. 10. A.
11. B. 12. A. 13. B. 14. B. 15. A. 16. B. 17. A. 18. [fluːxən]. 19. [zɛks]. 20. [ʃʏts].
21. [vaks]. 22. [lɪçts]. 23. [rɛçən]. 24. [karaktər]. 25. [melaŋkoːlɪʃ]. 26. [tsɛtsiːi̯ə].

Name _____

WORKSHEET NO. 9 : Chapter 7,   General Review

Transcribe each word. This list contains a few words that do not follow the normal rules. If you do not understand the answer, use the index in *Gateway to German Diction* to find the relevant explanation or look up the word in a dictionary.

1. *ihnen* (to them)   [_____]

2. *die Lieder* (songs)   [_____]

3. *immer* (always)   [_____]

4. *blicke* (look!)   [_____]

5. *die Erde* (earth)   [_____]

6. *der See* (lake)   [_____]

7. *erspähen* (to spy)   [_____]

8. *die Väter* (fathers)   [_____]

9. *die Männer* (men)   [_____]

10. *zerreißen* (tear up)   [_____]

11. *betten* (to bed down)   [_____]

12. *die Saat* (sowing)   [_____]

13. *der Abend* (evening)   [_____]

14. *verachten* (to scorn)   [_____]

15. *anziehen* (to dress)   [_____]

16. *loben* (to praise)   [_____]

17. *hoch*   (high)   [_____]

18. *kommen* (to come)   [_____]

19. *das Loch* (hole)   [_____]

20. *der Schuh* (shoe)   [_____]

21. *das Buch* (book)   [_____]

22. *beruht* (is based)   [_____]

23. *darum* (around which)   [_____]

24. *der Schlummer* (slumber)   [_____]

25. *rühmen* (to laud)   [_____]

26. *truebe* (dark, gloomy)   [_____]

27. *die Mütter* (mothers)   [_____]

28. *fluestern* (to whisper)   [_____]

29. *die Söhne* (sons)   [_____]

30. *der Loewe* (lion)   [_____]

31. *die Löcher* (holes)   [_____]

32. *öfters* (quite often)   [_____]

33. *leider* (unfortunately)   [_____]

34. *der Jäger* (hunter)   [_____]

35. *der Traum* (dream)   [_____]

36. *die Aue* (river meadow)   [_____]

37. *träumen* (to dream)   [_____]

38. *bereuen* (to regret)   [_____]

39. *ob* (whether)   [_____]

40. *das Rad* (wheel)   [_____]

41. *erregt* (excited)   [_____]

42. *wegjagen* (to drive away)   [_____]

43. *endllch* (at last)   [_____]

44. *das Mädchen* (girl)   [_____]

45. *sacht* (quietly)   [_____]

46. *recht* (right)   [_____]

47. *horcht* (heeds)   [_____]

48. *der Fuchs* (fox)   [_____]

49. *der Opernchor* (opera chorus)   [_____]

50. *bebt* (trembles)   [_____]

51. *die Stücke* (pieces)   [_____]

52. *todt* (dead)   [_____]

53. *der Berg* (mountain)   [_____]

54. *der König* (king)   [_____]

55. *königlich* (royal)   [_____]

56. *gehabt* (had)   [_____]

57. *ehe* (before)   [_____]

58. *die Einheit* (unity)   [_____]

59. *der Sänger* (singer)   [_____]

60. *dünkt* (seems)   [_____]

61. *das Pferd* (horse)   [_____]

62. *quaelen* (to torment)   [_____]

63. *die Sehnsucht* (longing)   [_____]

64. *der Hals* (neck)   [_____]

65. *die Jahreszeit* (season)   [_____]

66. *die Trübsal* (misery)   [_____]

67. *fester* (more solid)   [_____]

68. *der Busch* (bush)   [_____]

69. *gespannt* (eager)   [_____]

70. *gestehen* (to confess)   [_____]

71. *erste* (first)   [_____]

72. *Thomas* (name)   [_____]

73. *klatschen* (to clap)   [_____]

74. *der Satz* (sentence)   [_____]

75. *der Volkswagen* (people's car) [_____]

ANSWERS: 1. [i̱ːnən]. 2. [li̱ːdər]. 3. [ɪ̱mmər]. 4. [bli̱kə]. 5. [e̱rːdə]. 6. [ze̱ː]. 7. [ɛrʃpɡ̱ːən]. 8. [fɡ̱ːtər].
9. mɛ̱nnər. 10. [ʦɛrra̱esən]. 11. [bɡ̱tən]. 12. [za̱ːt]. 13. [ɑ̱ːbənt]. 14. [fɛrʔa̱xtən]. 15. [a̱ntsiːən]. 16. [lo̱ːbən].
17. [ho̱ːx]. 18. [ko̱mmən]. 19. [lɔx]. 20. [ʃuː]. 21. [buːx]. 22. [bəru̱ːt]. 23. [daru̱m]. 24. [ʃlu̱mmər].
25. [ryːmən]. 26. [tryːbə]. 27. [my̱ter]. 28. [fly̱stərn]. 29. [zøːnə]. 30. [løːvə]. 31. [lœçər]. 32. [œ̱ftərs].
33. [la̱edər]. 34. [jɡ̱ːgər]. 35. [traom]. 36. [aoo̱]. 37. [trɔ̱ømən]. 38. [bərɔ̱ø̱ən]. 39. [ɔp]. 40. [ra̱ːt].
41. [ɛrre̱ːkt]. 42. [vɛkja̱ːgən]. 43. [ɡ̱ntlɪç]. 44. [mɡ̱ːtçən]. 45. [zaxt]. 46. [rɛçt]. 47. [hɔrçt]. 48. [fʊks].
49. [o̱ːpərnkoːr]. 50. [be̱ːpt]. 51. [ʃty̱kə]. 52. [to̱ːt]. 53. [bɛrk]. 54. [køːnɪç]. 55. [køːnɪklɪç]. 56. [gəha̱ːpt].
57. [e̱ːə]. 58. [a̱enhaet]. 59. [zɡ̱nər]. 60. [dy̱ŋkt]. 61. [pfeːrt]. 62. [kvɡ̱ːlən]. 63. [ze̱ːnzʊxt]. 64. [hals].
65. [ja̱rəstsaet]. 66. [try̱ːpzaːl]. 67. [fɡ̱stər]. 68. [bʊʃ]. 69. [gəʃpa̱nt]. 70. [gəʃte̱ːən]. 71. [e̱ːrstə].
72. [to̱ːmas]. 73. [kla̱tʃən]. 74. [zats]. 75. [fɔ̱lksvaːgən].

Name _____

Listening Assignment

Choose a recording of some song from your anthology, preferably one that you want to learn.
If possible, choose a native German singer of the same voice category as your own.
Listen thoughtfully several times and answer the questions below.
(Most of the questions ask for your opinions; there are no possible wrong answers.)
If you can find the same song recorded by other singers, listen to them also and make comparisons.

Title of the song: _____

Composer: _____

Singer's name: _____

Pianist's name: _____

Title of the CD: _____

Manufacturer and number: _____

Which (if any) phonemes, either vowels or consonants, sound different from the way you expected them to sound?

Which words receive a particular emphasis? What kind of emphasis?

Does the singer make any phrasing choices that surprise you? Will you phrase the same way?

Where (if at all) does the singer make a change in tone color? Is the change related to text meaning?

What is your overall impression of this performance?

Transcription Exercise

Name _____

Poem by Joseph von Eichendorff (1788–1857).
Set to music by Robert Schumann (1810–1856)
in *Liederkreis* (*Song Cycle*), Opus 39.

"Mondnacht" (*"Moon Night"*) [mo̲:ntnaxt]
It seemed as if heaven had silently kissed the earth, so that, amid gleaming blossoms, it could dream of nothing else. A breeze passed over the field, stirring the stalks of grain, the forest rustled lightly, the starry night was clear. And my soul spread wide its wings and flew over the quiet land, as if it were flying toward home.

[_____]

Es war, als hätt der Himmel
It was as had the sky

[_____]

Die Erde still geküsst,
the earth quietly kissed,

[_____]

Dass sie im Blütenschimmer
so-that it (earth) in blossom-glistening

[_____]

Von ihm nun träumen müsst.
of it now dream had-to.

[_____]

Die Luft ging durch die Felder,
The breeze passed through the fields,

[_____]

Die Ähren wogten sacht,
the ears-of-grain swayed softly,

[_____]

Es rauschten leis die Wälder,
it rustled softly the forests,

[_____]

So sternklar war die Nacht.
so star-clear was the night.

[_____]

Und meine Seele spannte
And my soul spread

[_____]

Weit ihre Flügel aus,
wide its wings out,

[_____]

Flog durch die stillen Lande,
flew through the quiet fields

[_____]

Als flöge sie nach Haus.
as flew it toward home

KEY: Transcription Exercise

"Mondnacht" (*"Moon Night"*) [mo̱:ntnaxt]

[ɛs wɑːr als ɔp der hɪmməl _____]
     Es war, als hätt der Himmel

[diː eːrdə ʃtɪl geky̱st _____]
     Die Erde still geküsst,

[das ziː ɪm bly̱ːtənʃɪmmər _____]
     Dass sie im Blütenschimmer

[fɔn iːm nuːn trɔømən myst _____]
     Von ihm nun träumen müsst.

[diː lʊft gɪŋ dʊrç diː fɛldər _____]
     Die Luft ging durch die Felder,

[diː ɛːən voːktən zaxt _____]
     Die Ähren wogten sacht,

[ɛs rɑoʃtən laez diː vɛldər _____]
     Es rauschten leis die Wälder,

[zoː ʃtɛrnklɑːr wɑrː diː naxt _____]
     So sternklar war die Nacht.

[ʊnt mae̱nə zeːlə ʃpa̱ntə _____]
     Und meine Seele spannte

[vaet i̱ːrə fly̱ːgəl ɑos _____]
     Weit ihre Flügel aus,

[floːk dʊrç diː ʃtɪllən la̱ndə _____]
     Flog durch die stillen Lande,

[als flo̱ːgə ziː nax hɑos _____]
     Als flöge sie nach Haus.

Name _____

QUIZ: Chapter 1   / 10 Points

Match the following terms with their definitions.
One term will be left over (not matched).

A. Affricate

1. _____   In the middle; between vowels

B. Allophone

2. _____   Speech sound made with unobstructed breath

C. Consonant

3. _____   Word with same spelling, different meaning

D. Diphthong

4. _____   Written aspect of language

E. Homonym

5. _____   Brief vowel that is perceived as a consonant

F. Medial

6. _____   Speech sound accepted as equivalent to another

G. Orthography

7. _____   Science of speech sounds

H. Phonemes

8. _____   Speech sound made with interference to the breath

I. Phonetics

9. _____   Combination of a stop consonant and a fricative

J. Semivowel

10. _____   Complex speech sound that includes two vowels

K. Vowel

Name _____

QUIZ: Chapter 2   / 7 Points

1. English, German and Dutch belong to a family of languages known as _____.

2. Another language that belongs to that family is _____.

3. The English translation of *Hochdeutsch* is _____.

4. The English translation of *Bühnendeutsch* is _____.

5. Modern German evolved from the German style that

    Martin Luther developed when he translated _____

6. Prior to 1950, most "loan words" came into the

    German language from Greek, Latin and _____.

7. "Siebs" and "Duden" are reference sources

    that we use to find out correct German _____.

Name _____

QUIZ: Chapter 3   / 8 Points

1–4. Put a plus sign "+" by qualities that are characteristic of German and other Germanic languages.
Put a zero "0" by qualities that are non-existent or weak in German.

Energetic pronunciation of consonants   _____

Open syllables (ending with vowels)   _____

Smooth, legato connection between syllables   _____

Strong syllable stress   _____

5. English, German and Dutch all include several

   aspirated sounds, for example, the consonant   [____]

6. The most basic and important element of a word is called the _____

7. When two words are joined together, the result is called a _____

8. The IPA symbol [ʔ] stands for a syllable separation that may

   be called by the term _____

Name _____

QUIZ: Chapter 4   / 10 Points

Is the underlined vowel long (**L**) or short (**S**)?

1. b<u>i</u>tte (I ask)   _____

2. das W<u>o</u>rt (word)   _____

3. das P<u>aa</u>r (pair)   _____

4. der S<u>o</u>hn (son)   _____

5. l<u>ie</u>ber (dear)   _____

6. <u>o</u>ft (often)   _____

7. h<u>a</u>ben (to have)   _____

8. s<u>u</u>mmen (to hum)   _____

True (**T**) or False (**F**)?

9. German composers consistently use shorter note values for

   short vowels and longer ones for long vowels.   _____

10. The IPA symbol [ː] means that the preceding vowel is lengthened.   _____

Name _____

QUIZ: Chapter 5, Vowels (except mixed vowels)   / 12 Points

Give the correct IPA symbol for the underlined vowel. Use [ː] after every long vowel.

1. die Mutter (mother) [___]   2. ihnen (to them)   [___]

3. wehen (to blow)   [___]   4. nah (near)   [___]

5. dich (thee, obj.)   [___]   6. der Ball (ball)   [___]

7. zu (to)   [___]   8. gewonnen (has won) [___]

9. das Boot (boat)   [___]   10. die Krähe (crow)   [___]

11. dämmern   [___]   12. des (the, poss.)   [___]
    (to grow dusky)

Name _____

QUIZ: Chapter 5, Mixed Vowels   / 12 Points

1. The IPA symbol [œ] stands for one sound of the German letter _____.

2. The IPA symbol [yː] stands for one sound of the German letter _____.

3. The IPA symbol [øː] stands for one sound of the German letter _____.

4. The IPA symbol [ʏ] stands for one sound of the German letter _____.

5. Compared to the tongue position for [ʏ],

   is the tongue position for [œ] higher or lower?   _____

6. Compared to the way the lips are rounded for [yː],

   are the lips rounded for [øː] smaller or larger?   _____

7. If your keyboard does not have the letter Ü, what can you write instead? _____

Give the correct IPA symbol for the underlined vowel. Use [ː] after every long vowel.

8. stöhnen (to groan) [____]   9. die Trümmer (rubble) [____]

10. kühl (cool)   [____]   11. die Vögel (birds)   [____]

12. öffentlich (public) [____]

Name _____

QUIZ: Chapter 6   / 7 Points

Choose the diphthong that occurs in each word: [ae, ɑo, ɔø]

1. schauen (to look)   [___]   2. Mai (May)   [___]

3. die Reue (regret)   [___]   4. der Baum (tree)   [___]

5. deine (your)   [___]   6. die Träume (dreams)   [___]

7. die Haeuser (houses)   [___]

Name _____

QUIZ: Chapter 7   / 16 Points

Complete the sentences.

1. In the spelling NK, the N might be pronounced [n] or   [____]

2. The only lateral consonant in German is   [____]

3. Certain voiced consonants become voiceless when final; they are B, D and   _____

4. This means that final B is pronounced   [____]

5. And final D is pronounced   [____]

6. In English, [f] can be spelled with F or with PH; in German, [f] can
   also be spelled with the letter   _____

7. In English, [v] is spelled with V; in German words, [v] is spelled with   _____

Give the correct IPA symbol for the INITIAL consonant.

8. sehr (very)   [____]

9. schief (sloping)   [____]

10. spinnen (to spin)   [____]

11. jauchzen (to shout for joy)   [____]

12. ziemlich (somewhat)   [____]

Give the correct IPA symbol for the FINAL consonant.

13. freudig (happy)   [____]

14. stach (stuck)   [____]

15. Herz (heart)   [____]

16. solch (such)   [____]

Quiz Answers

Quiz, Chapter 1: F. 2. K. 3. E. 4. G. 5. J. 6. B. 7. I. 8. C. 9. A. 10. D.
(Note: the letter H is not used as an answer.)

Quiz, Chapter 2: 1. Germanic. 2. (see p. 14). 3. High German. 4. Stage German. 5. the Bible. 6. French. 7. pronunciation.

Quiz, Chapter 3: 1. +. 2. 0. 3. 0. 4. +. 5. (one of:) [t p k h]. 6. root. 7. compound. 8. glottal stop.

Quiz, Chapter 4: 1. S. 2. S. 3. L. 4. L. 5. L. 6. S. 7. L. 8. S. 9. F. 10. T.

Quiz, Chapter 5, part 1: 1. [ʊ]. 2. [iː]. 3. [eː] 4. [ɑː] 5. [ɪ]. 6. [a]. 7. [uː] 8. [ɔ]. 9. [oː]. 10. [ɛː]. 11. [ɛ]. 12. [ɛ].

Quiz, Chapter 5, part 2: 1. Ö. 2. Ü. 3. Ö. 4. Ü. 5. lower. 6. larger. 7. UE. 8. [øː]. 9. [ʏ]. 10. [yː]. 11. [øː]. 12. [œ].

Quiz, Chapter 6: 1. [ao]. 2. [ae]. 3. [ɔø]. 4. [ao]. 5. [ae]. 6. [ɔø]. 7. [ɔø].

Quiz, Chapter 7: 1. [ŋ]. 2. [l]. 3. G. 4. [p]. 5. [t]. 6. V. 7. W. 8. [z]. 9. [ʃ]. 10. [ʃ]. 11. [j]. 12. [ts]. 13. [ç]. 14. [x]. 15. [ts]. 16. [ç].

Name _____

FINAL EXAM: Part 1   Closed Book

TRUE (T) or FALSE (F)?

1. English is a Germanic language.   _____

2. *Hochdeutsch* is the language of government in Germany, Denmark and Holland.   _____

3. *Bühnendeutsch* is the dialect spoken in the Bühnen mountains.   _____

4. A standard German language grew out of Luther's translation of the Bible.   _____

5. Singers use some pronunciations that are out of fashion for daily conversation.   _____

6. H is always silent in German.   _____

7. German stop consonants, P, T and K, are aspirated as they are in English.   _____

Are the sounds represented by these IPA symbols used in ENGLISH only (**E**),
in GERMAN only (**G**), or BOTH (**B**)?

8. [w]   _____   9. [ç]   _____

10. [œ]   _____   11. [z]   _____

12. [ɪ]   _____   13. [æ]   _____

FILL IN THE BLANKS

14. Four German **bright** vowels are distinguished from each other by the position of the

_____. In order from the most closed to the most open, the bright vowels

are: [iː],   15. [____],   16. [____] and 17. [____].

18. Four German **dark** vowels are distinguished from each other by the position of the

_____. In order from the most closed to the most open, the dark vowels

are: [uː], 19. [____], 20. [____] and 21. [____].

The four German **mixed** vowels in order from the most closed to the most open are;

22. [____], [y], 23. [____] and 24. [____].

25 - 27. [ʏ] uses the tongue position of [____] and the lip position of [____]
        [ʏ] is one possible pronunciation of the letter   ____

28. The most important characteristic of the vowel [ə] is   _____

29. In German [ə] is always spelled with the letter   ____

Each word has been transcribed three times, but only one transcription is correct.
Put the letter of the correct transcription in the blank at the right.

30. der Sänger   A. [zɛ̱ŋər]   B. [za̱ŋgər]   C. [sɛ̱ŋgər]   _____
    (singer)

31. gedenken   A. [gedɛ̱ŋkən]   B. [gedɛ̱nkən]   C. [gədɛ̱ŋkən]   _____
    (to commemorate)

32. letzte   A. [lɛ̱tsɛ]   B. [lɛ̱tstə]   C. [lɛ̱ttsɛ]   _____
    (last)

33. der Knopf   A. [nɔpf]   B. [knɔpf]   C. [knɔf]   _____
    (button)

34. groß   A. [groːp]   B. [groːts]   C. [groːs]   _____
    (large)

35. die Qual   A. [kvɑːl]   B. [kwɑːl]   C. [quɑːl]   _____
    (agony)

36. Tasche   A. [ta̱ʃhɛ]   B. [ta̱çə]   C. [ta̱ʃə]   _____
    (pocket)

Which diphthong is in the word? [ae], [ɑo] or [ɔø]?

37. *treu* (true)   [____]

38. *der Traum* (dream)   [____]

39. *die Träume* (dreams)   [____]

40. *Prey* (famous baritone)   [____]

41. *Mai* (month of May)   [____]

How is *CH* pronounced in these words?

42. *die Sache* (thing)   [____]

43. *manche* (some)   [____]

44. *fluchen* (curse)   [____]

45. *nichts* (nothing)   [____]

How is *G* pronounced in these words?

46. *wenig* (little)   [____]

47. *weniger* (less)   [____]

48. *der Tag* (day)   [____]

49. How is *Z* always pronounced?   [____]

50. The word *"Wirtshaus"* contains the letter combination SH, but SH is not a typical

German spelling. What does this tell you about the word? _____

How is *S* pronounced in these words?

51. *gestehen* (confess)   [_____]

52. *die Nase* (nose)   [_____]

53. *Stimme* (voice)   [_____]

54. *des Tags* (day's)   [_____]

55. *beste* (best)   [_____]

56. *spielen* (play)   [_____]

57. *suchen* (seek)   [_____]

58. If your keyboard does not have *ß*, what can you use instead?   _____

59. If your keyboard does not have *ä*, what can you use instead?   _____

Optional Questions for EXTRA CREDIT — Transcribe

X1. Nibelungenlied   [_____]

X2. Das Rheingold   [_____]

X3. Götterdämmerung   [_____]

X4. Die Walküre   [_____]

ORAL EXAM

1. _____   7. _____

2. _____   8. _____

3. _____   9. _____

4. _____   10. _____

5. _____   11. _____

6. _____   12. _____

Final Score

Part 1, Closed Book   _____ /59 points

Part 2, Open Book   _____ /50 points

Oral Reading   _____ /24 points

Total   _____ /133 points

Percentage (total score divided by 133)   _____ %

Letter grade   _____

(Up to 4 Extra Credit points, if allowed, can make up for missed points in Parts 1 and 2.)

KEY: FINAL EXAM, Part 1   Closed Book

1. T. 2. F. 3. F. 4. T. 5. T.

6. F. 7. T. 8. E. 9. G. 10. G.

11. B. 12. B. 13. E. 14. tongue. 15. [ɪ].

16. [eː]. 17. [ɛ]. 18. lips. 19. [ʊ]. 20. [oː].

21. [ɔ]. 22. [yː]. 23. [øɪ] 24. [œ]. 25. [ɪ].

26. [ʊ]. 27. Ü. 28. unstressed. 29. E. 30. A.

31. C. 32. B. 33. B. 34. C. 35. A.

36. C. 37. [ɔø]. 38. [ɑo]. 39. [ɔø]. 40. [ae].

41. [ae]. 42. [x]. 43. [ç]. 44. [x]. 45. [ç].

46. [ç]. 47. [g]. 48. [k]. 49. [ts]. 50. it is a compound word.

51. [ʃ]. 52. [z]. 53. [ʃ]. 54. [s]. 55. [s].

56. [ʃ]. 57. [z]. 58. SS. 59. Ä.

X1. [niːbəlʊŋənliːt]. X2. [raengɔlt]. X3. [gœtərdɛmmərʊŋ]. X4. [valkyːrə].

FINAL EXAM: Part 2   Open Book

Name _____

This beautiful poem was set to music by Hermann Reutter (1900–1985) in *Neun Lieder* (1971).
Transcribe it into IPA. Indicate **long vowels**, such as [oː].
<u>Underline</u> the stressed syllable in <u>any</u> word with more than one syllable.

[_____]

Um   bei   dir zu sein,
In-order beside you to be   (To be with you,)

[_____]

Trüg'   ich Not   und Fährde,
would-bear I   necessity and danger,   (I would bear need and danger,)

[_____]

Ließ'   ich Freund und Haus
would-leave I   friend   and home   (I would leave friends and home,)

[_____]

Und die Fülle   der   Erde.
and   the fullness of-the earth.   (and all the earth.)

[_____]

Mich verlangt nach dir
I   long   for   you   (I long for you)

[_____]

Wie die Flut nach dem Strande,
as   the waves for   the   beach,   (as waves long for the shore,)

[_____]

Wie die Schwalbe im Herbst
as   the swallow   in autumn   (as a swallow in autumn)

[_____]

Nach dem südlichen Lande,
for   the   southern   land,   (longs for the South,)

[_____]

Wie den Alpsohn heim,
as   the Alps-son home,   (as a mountain lad longs for home)

[_____]

Wenn er denkt, nachts alleine,
when   he thinks   at-night alone   (when he thinks, alone at night,)

[_____]

An die Berge   voll Schnee
about the mountains full-of snow   (about snow-covered mountains)

[_____]

Im   Mondenscheine.
in-the moonlight.   (in moonlight.)

by Ricarda Huch (1864–1947)

KEY: FINAL EXAM, Part 2 Open Book

(Note: Certain variations are permissible as long as basic phonemes are present. The teacher must use discretion, considering how much class time has been available and how much detailed knowledge can be expected.)

Suggested method of scoring: 1 point for each correct syllable.
No score for duplicated words or syllables, indicated below by ___ .

Scoring Key:

Um bei dir zu sein	5	[ʊm bae diːr ʦuː zaen]
Trüg' ich Not und Fähr-de	6	[tryːk ɪç noːt ʊnt fɛ̱ːrde]
Ließ ' ___ Freund ___ Haus	3	[liːs' ___ frɔønt ___ hɑos]
___ die Fül-__ der Er-__	4	[___ diː fy̱l-__ der e̱ːr-__]
Mich ver- langt nach ___	4	[mɪç fɛrlaŋt nax ___]
Wie ___ Flut ___ dem Stran-__	4	[viː ___ fluːt ___ dem ʃtra̱n-__]
___ ___ Schwal-__ im Herbst	3	[___ ___ ʃva̱l-__ ɪm hɛrpst]
___ ___ süd-lich-en Lan-__	4	[___ ___ zyːtlɪçən la̱n-__]
___ ___ Alp-sohn heim	3	[___ ___ a̱lpzoːn haem]
wenn er denkt nachts al-lei-__	6	[vɛn er dɛŋkt naxts alla̱e-__]
An ___ Ber-ge voll Schnee	5	[an ___ bɛ̱rgə fɔl ʃneː]
___ Mon-den-schei-__	3	[___ mo̱ːndənʃae-__]

Total	50 points

PART 3: Oral Reading from a Word List

[Suggestions for administration: The student reads aloud, full voice, and reads each word twice. A word spoken correctly twice scores 2 points. A word spoken incorrectly the first time and correctly the second time scores 1 point. In order to conduct the oral exam while other students are present, the list can be partially randomized by changing the order of the pages and by instructing the student to begin at a certain number and to read only odd numbered or only even numbered words. The IPA transcription given on the right can be hidden by folding the paper, at the discretion of the teacher.]

1. der Schatz
   (treasure) [ʃats]

2. flüstern
   (to whisper) [flʏstərn]

3. recht
   (right) [rɛçt]

4. erregt
   (excited) [ɛrreːkt]

5. leider
   (unfortunately) [laedər]

6. hoch
   (high) [hoːx]

7. dieMänner
   (men) [mɛnnər]

8. der Schuh
   (shoe) [ʃuː]

9. dünkt
   (seems) [dʏŋkt]

10. die Stücke
    (pieces) [ʃtʏkə]

11. gespannt
    (eager) [gəʃpant]

12. sacht
    (quietly) [zaxt]

13. das Loch
    (hole) [lɔx]

14. die Königin
    (queen) [køːnɪgɪn]

15. ausheben
    (to lift out) [aoheːbən]

16. jagen
    (to hunt) [jɑːgən]

17. Schoenberg
    (composer's name) [ʃøːnbɛrk]

18. brausen
    (to roar) [braozən]

19. zerreißen
    (to tear apart) [tsɛrraesən]

20. bereuen
    (to repent) [bərɔøən]

21. die Väter
    (fathers) [fɛːtər]

22. Blumenstrauß
    (bouquet) [bluːmənʃtraos]

23. die Maid
    (maiden) [maet]

24. der Pfeil
    (arrow) [pfael]

25. horcht   [hɔrçt]
(listens)

26. der Leib   [laep]
(body)

27. der Löwe   [lø:və]
(lion)

28. trübe   [try:bə]
(gloomy)

29. die Trübsal   [try:pzɑːl]
(misery)

30. der Busch   [buʃ]
(bush)

31. die Söhne   [zø:nə]
(sons)

32. der Liebe   [li:bə]
(love's)

33. anziehen   [antsi:ən]
(to put on clothing)

34. die Löcher   [løçər]
(holes)

35. versäumen   [fɛrzɔømən]
(to miss)

36. erspähen   [ɛrʃpɛːən]
(to spy)

37. die Lieder   [[li:dər]
(songs)

38. das Wirtshaus [vɪrtshɑos]
(tavern)

39. quälen   [kvɛ:lən]
(to torment)

40. rühmen   [ry:mən]
(to praise)

41. öfters   [œftərs]
(oftentimes)

42. die Mutter   [mʊttər]
(mother)

43. verachten   [fɛrʔaxtən]
(to scorn)

44. beruht   [bəru:t]
(is based)

45. der Jäger   [jɛ:gər]
(hunter)

46. der Schütz   [ʃyts]
(shooter)

47. hinab   [hɪnap]
(downward)

48. innen   [ɪnnən]
(inside)

49. richten   [rɪçtən]
(to set upright)

50. die Höhe   [hø:ə]
(high place)

51. ersticken   [ɛrʃtɪkən]
(to choke)

52. des Weges   [dɛs ve:gəs]
(the way's)

53. beruhigt   [bəru̱ːɪçt]
(reassures)

54. der Weg   [veːk]
(the way)

55. die Götter   [gœtər]
(gods)

56. der Ochs   [ɔks]
(ox)

57. ihnen   [iːnən]
(to them)

58. wir   [viːɾ]
(we)

59. die Musik   [muziːk]
(music)

60. vielleicht   [fila̱eçt]
(perhaps)

61. das Gebet   [gəbe̱ːt]
(high)

62. die Minne   [mɪnnə]
(love)

63. hättest   [hɛtəst]
(if you had)

64. hässlich   [hɛslɪç]
(ugly)

65. die Jagd   [jɑːkt]
(hunting)

66. obwohl   [ɔpvo̱ːl]
(although)

67. der Mond   [moːnt]
(moon)

68. oben   [o̱ːbən]
(up above)

69. unruhig   [ʊnruːɪç]
(restless)

70. weg   [vɛk]
(away)

71. die Ruhe   [ru̱ːə]
(quietness, rest)

72. dafür   [dafy̱ːɾ]
(for that)

73. stürzen   [ʃtʏrtsən]
(to plunge downward)

74. flötet   [fløːtət]
(to play or sound like a flute)

75. höchstens   [hø̱ːçstəns]
(at the most)

76. löschen   [lœʃən]
(to quench)

77. wärst   [vɛːrst]
(if-you-were)

78. schleicht   [ʃlaeçt]
(creeps)

79. das Taubenpaar   [ta̱obənpɑːr]
(pair of doves)

80. scheut   [ʃɔøt]
(avoids)

81. das Gesträuch [gəʃtrɔøç]
(shrubbery)

82. die Pforte [pfɔrtə]
(gate)

83. der Psalm [psalm]
(psalm)

84. hübsch [hʏpʃ]
(pretty)

85. der Chorleiter [koːrlaetər]
(choral conductor)

86. die Qual [kvɑːl]
(agony)

87. der Knabe [knɑːbə]
(lad)

88. die Gnade [gnɑːdə]
(grace, mercy)

89. brav [brɑːf]
(well-behaved)

90. das Veilchen [faelçən]
(violet)

91. die Wehmut [veːmuːt]
(melancholy)

92. am frühesten [am fryːəstən]
(at the earliest)

93. die Seele [zeːlə]
(soul)

94. die Quellen [kvɛlən]
(springs of water)

95. das Schauspiel [ʃɑoʃpiːl]
(stageplay)

96. zerstreut [tsɛrʃtrɔøt]
(scattered)

97. der Zecher [tsɛçər]
(drinker)

98. das Märchen [mɛːrçən]
(fairy tale)

99. verjüngt [fɛrjʏŋt]
(made young again)

100. rauchen [rɑoxən]
(to smoke)

101. du lachst [duː laxst]
(you laugh)

102. der Wunsch [vʊnʃ]
(wish)

103. himmelhoch [hɪməlhoːx]
(as high as heaven)

104. das Mädchen [mɛːtçən]
(girl)

105. die Mütter [mʏttər]
(mothers)

106. dunkel [dʊŋkəl]
(dark)

107. rhythmisch [rʏtmɪʃ]
(rhythmical)

Performance Evaluation Sheet

Song Title: _____   Name _____

SELF-GRADE FOR STYLE AND EXPRESSION   _____

TEACHER'S GRADE FOR STYLE AND EXPRESSION   _____

    Phrasing for meaning?

    Dynamics?

    Energy level?

    Presentation?

    Correct rhythms ?

    Memorization?

SELF-GRADE FOR DICTION   _____

TEACHER'S GRADE FOR DICTION   _____

    Vowels: Correct?

        Clear?

    Diphthongs: Correct?

        Clear?

    Consonants: Correct?

        Energized?

DICTION ERRORS NOTED:

    In the word: the sound heard was: and it should have been: